A MOVING LANDSCAPE

First edition March 2009

First Published Great Britain 2009
by Summertime Publishing

ISBN 978-1-904881-17-9

Printed by LightningSource

Designed by www.creationbooth.com

Images:
Cover: Sam Parfitt
Author photograph: Daphne Johnson www.lucidpics.com
Other photographs:
England: Jo Parfitt and Patrick Gosling www.patrickgosling.com,
France: Ian Parfitt; Dubai: Ian Parfitt; Oman: Ian Parfitt;
Norway: Ian Parfitt

Grow Your Own Networks

Authors: Jo Parfitt and Jacqui Tillyard
Publisher: Summertime Publishing

Release the Book Within

Author: Jo Parfitt
Publisher: Lean Marketing Press

Career in Your Suitcase

Author: Jo Parfitt
Publisher: Lean Marketing Press

Expat Entrepreneur

Author: Jo Parfitt
Publisher: Lean Marketing Press

Find Your Passion

Author: Jo Parfitt
Publisher: Lean Marketing Press

How to be a Global Grandparent

Authors: Peter Gosling and Anne Huscroft with Jo Parfitt
Publisher: Zodiac Publishing

Dates

Authors: Jo Parfitt and Sue Valentine
Publisher: Zodiac Publishing

DEDICATION

To Ian, without whom my landscape would have simply stayed the same.

The sun is like a berry on a bush

So big and bright,

like a red-faced man.

Then a bird comes along and swallows it,

like the night coming in and the world is blind.

Patrick Gosling 1972 aged 8

CONTENTS

OMAN

NORWAY

ENGLAND

THE NETHERLANDS

ACKNOWLEDGEMENTS

My family is responsible for much of what made me who I am, of course. My mother, Jenny Gosling, has shown me through her passion for walking in autumn woods and along lonely shorelines and for painting what matters, that nature is a never-ending source of inspiration and joy. My father, Peter, has written 32 books and shown me that writing does count as a real career, when, aged 55, he gave up a life in teaching to write fulltime. My brother, Patrick, a photographer, proves, a second generation on, that creativity is everything. He had the audacity to beat me to my writing dreams by coming first in a competition, aged just eight, when I did not win anything until four years later, at fifteen, with Armagh. It is for this reason that his poem comes first in this anthology.

But, I must also thank June Counsel, children's author, who, in 1986, gave me my first introduction to creative writing. She told me back then that I was a poet, though I did not believe her. And to Annie Burgh, the novelist, who reawakened my love for writing fiction 20 years later when she led a wonderful class at Castle of Park in Scotland that changed my life. Annie reminded me to believe in myself and put me firmly and good-humouredly back on track.

Thanks are due, especially, to the committee of the Families in Global Transition conference, who gave me the courage to share my poetry in my closing keynote at the 2007 conference in Houston. It was only when I received a standing ovation that I realised, at last, that maybe my poetry was okay. And so specific thanks have to go to my writing muses, Robin Pascoe, Christine Yates, Apple Gidley, Jane Minshall, Carolyn van Es-Vines, Sue Southwood, and Annie's Golden Piglets who continually make me believe I can. And to Mary van der Boon, who first asked me to write this book.

Our children, Sam and Josh, never cease to inspire me and I thank them for accepting me for who I am, even though the ironing mountain is too frequently on the landscape.

This book has been compiled because this month my parents celebrate their Golden Wedding and I have finally run out of excuses not to publish the poetry they always encouraged me to write, read and recite. Thank you.

FOREWORD

When Jo asked me if I would write a foreword to her moving book of poetry about, well, moving, I agreed immediately as long as I didn't need to produce any poetry myself.

My request was a matter of pride. I knew I couldn't possibly produce any poetry of my own and certainly none the calibre of Jo's. I had heard her read some of her poems when she included a few as part of her rousing closing keynote address at the conference Families in Global Transition in Houston in 2007. I simply couldn't believe that her vast repertoire of writing styles on career mobility, on becoming a writer, an entrepreneur, even about cooking dates, could possibly also include poetry. How unfair, I thought, green with envy, that she could so passionately describe the experience of the shifting backgrounds of mobile lives in a form most would consider completely unconventional.

But Jo is all about passion, whether it be for the spouses she meets in her travels and workshops, for her colleagues and fellow writers, for her husband and sons, or for her parents whose Golden Wedding anniversary she so eloquently celebrates with this collection.

Her poems are evocative of not only a rich life, but one that is much appreciated too. As readers, we can be grateful her parents have reached the half century mark in their marriage so that we are now able to enjoy and celebrate with her family, so many lives that continue to be well-lived.

Robin Pascoe
www.expatexpert.com

INTRODUCTION

When I was seven year's old I wrote my first poem. It was called 'The Breeze am I' and my teacher liked it so much she asked me to read it out to the whole class. It felt good, standing there in front of a sea of upturned faces. And while, primarily, I write for me, I recognise that being able to share my words with others is a privilege that brings me joy.

Forty years after that classroom moment I am proud to have published 26 books and hundreds of articles. Few people are aware that poetry was my first love and that it has sustained me throughout my life. No other form of writing can penetrate so deeply, nor expose the writer so totally and excruciatingly. Perhaps that is why it has taken me so long to dare to share the words you now have in your hands.

As you read this collection you will watch the story of my life unfold as you take a journey that begins with my schooldays in Stamford, Lincolnshire, when we spent many childhood holidays on the North Norfolk coast. From there I moved to Hull University where I found my husband, Ian, and took the French degree that took me to Normandy. On graduating, I moved to London where I managed to fail at more jobs than I could count until I landed, aged 25, on the career that I have clung onto ever since. Being a freelance writer.

When, in 1986, Ian took a job in a place I had never heard of called Dubai, I moved back to Stamford for a while and learned to love nearby Rutland, where my parents have now lived for more than 20 years. Read the dates and places on the poems and you will discover the path my life has taken since, as I moved to Dubai, had my children, Sam and Josh, and the realisation dawned that a life on the move was there to stay. In 1993, Ian's company posted us to Oman. It is Arabia that ignited my imagination as is clear from the many poems I wrote during close to ten glorious years there. It was during these years that we enjoyed several holidays in the Far East. In 1996 we moved to Norway for a while before repatriating to Stamford for seven years just 18 months later. Finally, in late 2004, we moved to a small town outside The Hague in The Netherlands. Today, Sam and Josh are 16 and 17 and in a couple of years we will be moved on again.

Nature is important to me, as you will learn from the many poems that eulogise its beauty and borrow its metaphors for my experiences. My life has been a series of moves within a shifting scene of landscapes, and each landscape has moved me to write.

For this I am eternally grateful.

ENGLAND 1961 – 1981

Armagh

Amidst the desolation,
destruction and despair
in the County of Armagh,
people have to stay aware.
Though how can they forget
the pain and misery they endure,
when all they want is to be together,
stay secure?

Bullets fall.
Some shatter panes.
The gunman knows
that he's to blame.
The broken hearts
and ruined homes
prove that no-one
grieves alone.

People notice little things
In this battle no-one wins.

It helps to lift the rising death toll
when a little boy is playing football.

People notice little things
in this battle no-one wins.

Lincolnshire, February 1976

FRANCE 1981 – 1982

Castang

Pebble-dashed.
Only evil women are stoned
on stolen wine and skimming cailloux.

The dragonfly
on wings of azure
settled for a while
on the hearts of twelve disciples of happiness.

There is no progress
in swimming against the current bliss.

On me chatouille
avec une mauvaise herbe.
Je n'en veux pas.
En vacances on ne cueillit que les belles fleurs.

Dordogne, August 1981

Landscape

Hills lie breathless
between Nature's buttonholes
and man's ways.

Pine forests reach up
to the rainy sky.
Mammalian hair
on muddy earth.
Switchback.
Uphill downhill
winding weaving.
Slow down.
This is Normandy.

The game shelters
in the dank fern,
stealing refuge
from man's weals.

Back to earth.
Timber frames
fringed with thatch,
strengthened with mud.
Lifegiving land
with hills of hope
and valleys of security.

Normandy, November 1981

The rabbit we ate with mushrooms

The rabbit we ate with mushrooms
was lying on the kitchen table
twelve hours before.
I saw him.
Those furry ears, soft coat and downy tail,
silent, at peace.
His eyes were bright
but his last life's blood
dripped from his neck,
split after the blow.
They cut his skin above the knee
then ripped it to his hips.
Slowly, his coat was pulled up and over his head
and thrown into a bucket,
soon to be joined by stomach, entrails, heart and lungs.
The cat ate the insides for supper –
we ate the plump flesh with mushrooms.

Normandy, January 1982

A parody

Blind drunk.
Only blue women
cannot see the splinter
in their own eye
for it's bathed with hope.

The flighty dove
on wings of steel
deposed the heart of
the doubting one.
The tide itself chooses
when it will turn.

On me gratte avec
l'épine d'une rose fanée.
Je n'en veux pas.
En réalité
les plus belles fleurs sont empoisonées.

Normandy, June 1982

ENGLAND 1982-1987

Ambition

Nature's heralds swirl in space,
their delight expresses
the essence of my vagrant thoughts.
My aspirations strain to touch the crescendo
of their voice,
yet it is my heart
that wins the race,
leaping from my earthbound soul,
it brushes the apogee of the whim.
I will become great –
when the lark descends
or when I rise to greet the lark.

Norfolk, July 1982

Thornham

How romantic
to watch the rising tide
by twilight.

Down by the coal barn,
mooring posts beckon,
venture forward.
Silhouettes against a fading sky.
Blue grey haze
and lapping sea.
Rushes touching,
sway together,
alternately lauding
land and sea.

Stand and marvel
at the sounds of night.
Creeping tide,
soft calling larks.
The wind tells tales
of sailors lost beneath the waves
and forgotten trawlers,
shoals of lapping fish
and mussel nets.
Salt pervades the dusky air.
I lick my lips to savour
affinity with Nature,
cool against my ageing skin
and seeping through the pores
to touch my hungry soul.

Inland, the shore lights sparkle
but cannot snuff my joy
at knowing secrets of the night.
So still
I stand and stare.

Norfolk, July 1982

Wisbech

Fat houses sit squat,
crosslegged, hands on knees,
beside the Washward water's edge.
Some have waited patiently, hopelessly,
and their dead eyes look out of soulless skulls.
Others have had their dancing day,
now limp along, half-starved, dry-docked.
Ironically the prolific lairs
portray a happy, thriving air.
Their bellies full,
untouched by trade,
Virginia creeps along their chests.
Green carpet leads them to the dormant road
that takes no cargo to these portals.

Norfolk, July 1982

The Norfolk set

Girls sit on walls,
lounge on benches,
dawdle ten minutes
before the bus.
They live in tiny terraces,
white faces with green tongues of lawn.

Gentlefolk sit on barstools,
lounge in Rolls or XJS,
drink Pimms
with cucumber and ice.
They sleep behind high walls
in an alcoholic dream.

Tourists sit on canvas deckchairs
or huddle round the Calor fire,
drinking tea from Melaware
or light ale from the tin.
They escape to dwell in homes on wheels,
boxes that help them feel at ease.

Wild fowl sit on cool sea lavender,
float on a tide that ebbs and flows,
hop from islands in the marshland
exclaiming thanks for a life of peace.
They sleep calm amidst the samphire,
shrouded by the salty mist.

Norfolk, July 1982

Titchwell

Rushes stand
kneedeep
in water,
sentry to
their nesting
wards.
An armful
of skyward
swans
forms an
arc of
Nature,
screaming
praise
and threats
to those
with
telescopic
eyes, who
live lives
of espionage.
A bunch
of hollowed
twigs
prove palace
to a homeless
gull.
The guards
stand still
their boots
too full
to chastise
predators.
Man picks
up the
chase
and plants
foreboding
signposts
to prohibit
evil –
thus proving
this idyllic
space of
Nature
to not be
natural
at all.

Norfolk, July 1982

Up Bubbles, Hunstanton

The gate is narrow, the price is dear
but chips and burger free of charge.
Blackclad bouncers lurk in cobwebbed corners.
The path to the bar is full of obstacles –
tattooed toughnuts, shady characters
with three stars or 'please cut here'
emblazoned on wide necks.
Half shy eyes pin you to embarrassment
for most lookers wear 'sold' stickers
concealed from the uninformed.
More fool the holidaymakers,
one misconstrued glance
at a better half
and spies jump from the dance floor
and book a date.
Outside. Later.
The patrolling Pandas, too scared
to venture closer.

If you're on the pick up and fail
to tempt a pretendant with your rara
above the pier,
then there's a second chance outside,
when all depart on the pilgrimage
to the chip shop.
Starry-eyed and hopeful
that tonight some knight in chainmail
will cleave them from the necessary prop
of the chippy wall
before the police do their duty.

Abandon hope all ye who enter here.
The clientele is so select,
that unless you have fists of steel –
the wages of sin could well be death.

Norfolk, July 1982

The violinist

The most beautiful man in the orchestra
wore his inky dinner suit and unpressed off-white shirt,
his warm smile paralleled in the black bow at his slim neck.
The initialled handkerchief
made the image so demure.
He wields the arch across the strings
of the shiny curved body
in unison with twenty other diametric strokes.
His music curled around his neck and two hundred thirsty mouths
drank down the lyrical beauty,
swirling like his circling crown.

The unstyled collage of muted greys and blues stood
backcloth to this prince of darkness.
He had no place at the forefront of the stage
yet stood on the platform
of my proportionism.
Mirrored in the sleek bird of prey,
with baton in his talented hand,
whitechested and blacktailed.

His bow, his body, sweep up and down,
carried on a tide of triumph,
repercussions of emotion impel the crescendo of the symphony.
Music fills the soul,
attempting to touch
the fragile place
where life and lyricism combine.

Hull, November 1982

Sin

Gold on gold,
legs laced tighter than a corset.
The female serpent weaves
about the wavering sword
in quest of forbidden fruit.
Who is the thin man in the bed?
Is his partner living in his head?
Unspoken truths are littered
behind lips sealed tighter
than the kiss.
Oh give me shimmering thread
to weave my web into
a beauteous tapestry for life.

Hull, December 1982

The graduate of 1983

You are one of many who strive to be different.
The smoke from your cigarette draws
the vagrant picture of your life
in your expressive hand.
Is the way to achieve greatness
always combined
with midnight wanderings,
sleepless, alcoholic nights,
crosslegged on floors,
bursts of laughter
or pessimism?

Bemoaning life's harshness,
you drag your feet from shared room
to Tube
to wine bar
or restaurant
where you satirically sweep to
gloating American Express cards,
ever pleasant in your stopgap career.

You are waiting for the world to shower you
with the affluence it gave your forefathers.
Don't wait.

Put down your self-pity and self-love.
Take the confidence from under your
unmade bed and beneath undusted settees.
Forget your dissatisfied soul.
When you cease play-acting
the world will start being your audience.

London, December 1983

Garden Cottage

Garden of delight, softly scoops down to the stream
of passing fantasies.
Trickle past stones of solidarity.
Security in peonies, waxy Eastern beauty,
bold bloodstreaked purity,
lush crimson, row on row.
Iris flag the blushing rose
that clings to ruddy ruined wall –
and through the arch, an alpine mound
sealed by Solomon in all his glory.
Lilies valley in overjoyed undergrowth
of fern and springs of cyclamen.
Pastel poppies sown by Nature,
who alone would dare to venture
on a project of this scale,
which tempts the eye and spurns the flail.

If I lie back among the baby's tears
I hear the laughter of children,
bows in hair, with pinafores and buttoned boots,
dodging, running, skipping to the hayloft,
hiding in the dovecote, picking lupins.
Armfuls of colour swimming with delirious delight.

Again I hold my breath; the pigeons call,
Summer's heralds join the symphony of song.
The fat squirrel, plump as a cat,
bends the boughs that break my heart with joy.

Silver birch with tinkling leaves
and willow wear my laurel crown.
'I declare the mountain ash, shall henceforth wear the purple sash!'
But kneel down to the Christmas rose
and rise to praise wisteria,
who winds around the ancient yew
and spills like lace down through its boughs.

The stone-built cottage stands aside,
modest since before the Fire,
and calmly stretching back its frame
displays the place that chose its name.

Rutland, June 1984

Processed words

Shall I Wang you a letter
and fold its floppy form
into a faultless execution
free from error, smudge and scorn?

Perhaps the Wordplex would
perplex me
and the Xerox clear reject me
from its ranks
of cross-trained Merlins
Phillipses and AES,
magicians with a memory bank,
skilled technicians of the text.

May I then merge my plaintive cry
with sweet words processed by and by?
If you can wait while my insertion
of devotion, by the cursor,
is completed
and the errors are deleted.

Underscore my failings,
print my assets bold.
Control KD
your love for me
until the screen goes cold.
For .bak I come
a menu master,
chef of files,
character crafter.

The Wang forgets no document,
it saves the words of this lament,
while daisies wheel and print my tale
on headed parchment, crisp and pale.

Now I command the Autoscore
to boldly state what went before.

Control KD
your love for me
P.

London, June 1984

Race you to the tree!

Suffocated
inside a Perspex box that runs on silent wheels on tiny tracks,
drags me to the tube and tips me out to push along the platform,
ascend the escalator – crushed between the other boxed-in worker ants.

Sitting at my desk
I feel stifled by the well-used air.
No escape.
No vents or cracks.
Impervious cruel cage.

Society lures us to this box
then clamps it shut for forty years.
And Lethe lies in coffee cups
that dull our minds and soothe our fears.

A shred of my imagination
peels away convention's skin,
lifts and flies to the tip of the tree.
Ambition.
Sentry to the gate of life.
I hear the clink of keys.
Temptation.
A snake coils around the trunk.
Do I hear a gallows laugh?

The child in me begins to climb.
Ascent towards ambition.
Aspiring to attain the highest branch.

Look up!
Creativity cannot grow surrounded by stale thoughts,
repeated actions, dark inside the commuter's cage.

Look higher! Look beyond!
Scatter convention's garb.

Race you to the tree!

London, December 1984

Underlying theme

Please come
make me your bride.
In years to come
we'll fill the church
with laughter
and the sound of violins,
swaying to the tune
of love born now
to flower when the seed is ripe.
Enough to spawn
a life of hope together?

Hold me by the river bank
and watch the Chater flow
beneath the golden, grass-flanked bridge
from love of sea to land.

Before we choose to tread this path
we'll play Pooh Sticks on the bridge –
games to while away the years
until we end the fight,
the race to the top of separate trees,
the summit is the same.
We'll run parallel paths
and victorious we'll reign
with just a space between us,
transparent as truth, fragile as life,
threatening us with convention.
Should we dare to blow it away?

It hovers there,
vulnerable as poppy flowers,
with promises of heaven or hell.
So leave it there to flutter –
like my heart.

Yet if we stretch our fingers
to touch across the wall,
we cling so tight
and dare not breathe
nor speak for fear of falling,
falling away,
down on our own.
Alone.

Oh lover,
with the sun in your face
and life in your grey eyes,
that dance and sing
a tune I wish to learn.
As soon as,
soon as,
you allow.
Oh Ian,
we could take our vows
and climb our trees,
play Pooh Sticks
on the bridge of time
and swim to sea together.

Rutland, May 1986

Amstel Oasis

Dubai is in the desert –
but it isn't dry.
The sun scorches the unnatural flora –
that still receives a constant flow.
Palm trees, dressed in sackcloth,
beg the sky for rain
and it appears,
creeping humbly round their feet,
embarrassed by the modern means by which it came.

Bougainvillea flames purple,
clinging sheepishly to the walls of concrete playrooms,
coyly boasting verdance from inadvertent hoses.

Cranes and workmen build the ponds, the hills, the fast lanes,
planting grass greener that it ever shall be on the other side,
for it is fed and watered by some Sheikh's almighty hand.

Employment is international.
Only the blind beggar in his pram
needs hold out his hand.

Work while you are well.
The welfare state will never grow from lack of taxes.
While you are well there's a way to earn your bread –
be it pittance or golden-baked.

The world meets here.
Inside first class hotels,
lounging on the sundeck,
sipping Pimms through straws.
For here are exhibition halls,
conference rooms and swimming pools,
saunas, clubs and pubs.
Here is the home of the alcohol licence.
Here is the home of the Amstel can.

If you watch quietly,
you will see the Englishmen
neatly tuck their bellies into their trouser tops
and slowly fix their smiles and starry eyes
upon the taxi that takes them to their nightly wet dream.

Amstel Lite or Amstel plain?
We know when we will meet again
at Thatchers, Humphreys or the Falcon,
in the Odd Spot or Red Lion.
Tap your can to the music of the band,
live or pressed into a plastic disc,
or stretched inside a pirate tape
beside the video screen.

Home from home.
Without Saturday football by the telly,
feet on table, can on belly,
crisps crushed into the carpet
and lager to confuse the score.

Where is the real Dubai then?
Surely it cannot take the form of an Amstel swilling male
or a high thigh cut bikini strutting by the pool?
Then it must lurk behind those high walls and elegant gates,
flanked by oleander,
where the only peepshow comes from above.
Maybe this is where the dishdashed men and veiled women
carry out masked balls?

The people of the dhows cluster along Deiraside,
trading, transporting, carrying
on with life in a calm cross-legged way,
using their clothes as facecloths, then as towels,
shuffling towards their personal Nirvana,
wearing shapeless baggy suits,
commuting to the other side,
clinging like locusts to the abra's flesh.

Who will buy? Come and try. A look costs nothing
but we'll try to sell or haggle,
wash your car, be your barrow,
'Hello banana', 'Hello potato'.
Stallholders in the souk cry out for business,
polish up their apples, clean their peas and cues
and peel the skin from onions for humility.

Faded costumes, faded pride,
the locals step back to the shade,
conceal their thoughts and hide their heads,
leaving brightly coloured clothes for passing trade,
sitting on low stools they lunch on samosa and Cherryade
and accept that it is they who are the foreigners.
Private people with a private alphabet,
anonymous dress and hidden homes,
saving bright lights and splendour for the mosques
and their energy for lilting prayer
to cool the mind and fill the air.

Perhaps they laugh at the blatant follies
of the bronzing beer men,
arrogantly driving to distance themselves
from these boozing bar men,
cleverly retaining anonymity
behind the same beard and the same wry smile,
sardonic in its reverence of the red-faced, peeling white man,
rushing to catch the last can of Amstel.

Dubai, May 1986

To Christy Nolan

Thank you for your word-bunting,
dambursting through my mind,
tickling my thoughts
into action,
reminding me of the casserole
of words that I should
chop and splice
into a paper memory.

My pen never toils;
the pictures thick and fast
roll from my mind's eye
to the page
or tap tap tap
towards the screen.
There is no pain,
just freedom to spill
the beans
at breakneck speed.

Oh Christy,
how I feel your purpose
and your poise,
as stick-balancing you scribe.
It gives you time
to reflect,
to contemplate
and choose
each syllable and sound.

Your prose is poetry
and the rhythm found within
lulls me into assonance,
alliterates my thoughts,
stabs and teases
at my hand
until I join with you in rhyme.

Thank you for being
a match to me.
For you relit my waning flame
and prodded at my muse,
giving me rebirth.
My hope is neither heinous nor horrible
but sublime.
I'll pray for you
and thank the Lord
for giving life
to you.

It's true.
Writing is the transference of energy.

Rutland, June 1987

Winter

Tardy teardrops
pegged out in the fogfrost
drip daytime gold
downwards to the snowdust.
Crisp stillness
sliced only by the turtledove
as he dives from tree to wall
then wall to barn.
Stiffly starched
by November Sunday dawn.

The pane splits me from the sound
of a chestnut pony
clipping by,
so my eyes may compensate,
creating colours in his wake.

Handfuls of pyracantha
bomb the white with amber,
bullets berrydash
the lowly branches,
melt away their pearly shrouds,
bow their heads,
shrugging off the cold.

Slumbering bullrushes,
strangled by ice,
scarfed with cobwebs,
surrender their straight backs
attending spring.

Rutland, November 1987

Out in the cold

A stranger in my own body.
My skin, no longer mine
is pricked with gooseflesh.
My mind stifled.
Breath trapped in my chest.
A sigh starts in my forehead
and ends at my feet.
Nostrils flared,
raw and blazing with liquid fire.
My voice descends so low
that I cannot recognise it.
Each word throbs inside my ear.
Lips cracked.
Tongue parched.
Yet I have water.

Boiling potions soothe.
Too tired to move.
Yet sleep will not come.
Oh aching head,
oh smarting eyes,
freezing flesh
and firey frown
abate
and introduce me
to the self I knew
before this flu.

Rutland, November 1987

Granny gets into the swing

A fine 'feeding for the weeding'
at Hambleton Hall
with a view of Rutland Water,
the canapés were small,
the sofas inviting,
the décor exciting.
A fabulous treat for us all.

Then Granny got into the swing
of the thing and the alcohol went to her head.
'Don't let me go in a deck chair!
Please no, I couldn't take that.'
'I think you mean bath chair, dear Granny,'
we said and our faces started to crack.

Then Granny flopped into a chair
and said coffee wasn't for her,
but after a while, she reached for her cup.
It was empty
but she picked it up.
We laughed and insisted we fill it
with coffee and cream like you should,
then she drank from a spoon
and started to swoon
then shot back in her chair, like you would.

She cried when they brought in the cake though,
topped with sparklers
and there was a song.
It was more than our bellies could take though
but Granny agreed to have some
then chopped it to bits with her plate.
Then, cushion on lap,
had a panic attack.
Where was the clasp
to her bag then, she asked,
and wrestled in vain with the seam.

Convulsions took over the diners.
I had to dash out to the hall.
Thank goodness the taxi was waiting,
we'd get home in one piece after all.

Rutland, December 1987

The bride's speech

I'd always poo-pooed the idea
that once wooed
I'd jack in my job for a bloke.
But now it's occurred,
my career's been deferred
and my jetset ideas up in smoke.

'Tis rare that an ungainly goose
can trap a man without a noose,
wrench him from his wet suit,
make him fling away his fins,
discard his trusty depth gauge
and unstring his violin
for the ordinary life
of married man with quacking wife.

To leave the briny for the land
of compromise and holding hands
and 'yes dear, if you say so dear,'
tomorrow and tomorrow and tomorrow.

Will he prefer my nagging to the lure of oceans clear?
Will he miss the bachelor bliss
of a sandwich in the lift
after a night out on the beer?

For when this party's ended we must travel to the East,
we've decided to swim as Ian's got fins and I have my little webbed feet.
We are going to build our future amid dishdashes and mosques
with 'Allah wakbar' chanted, sunshine taken for granted,
bougainvillea planted, ruled by Sheikh Zayed bin Sultan al Nahyan, Supreme
Councillor, Ruler of Abu Dhabi and the United Arab Emirates
instead of Elizabeth our Queen.

I promise that I'll earn my keep
I'll bake and brew and mop and sweep
and make you little tempting snacks,
rub cocoa butter in your back.
But speaking as a living sacrifice –
I've never been happier in my life.

Rutland, December 1987

The day we left

And when day broke
it had not dawned
on man and wife
that their dreams
were now real life.
And while they supped
among old friends
their separateness no longer painful
but instead a joy
beyond belief.

But the goodbyes hurt,
the tears stung
to leave those who've proved
their love for many years
for someone still so new.
Conflicting emotions
break my heart.
Such joy, such gratitude.
Such bonds cannot be split
by miles and years.
The pain so hard to take
when sacrifice is theirs.
To leave behind
the loved ones,
the ones who really care.

Now I'll support two parties
yet cannot divide my time.
We waited too long.
Hello. Goodbye.
For every bride
rips into the reality.
She removes a smile to replace it with a tear.

Take off!
vve re away!
The love, the pain,
renewed
as memories.
So now to build that temple,
forge our pathway to the stars
not forgetting where we came from
and remembering the flowers in my bouquet.   *London, December 1987*

DUBAI 1987 – 1993

Nihil

Locked in.
Locked out.
Trapped inside
the thin red line
they call tape.

Stiff and starchy.
Unyielding faceless man.
No eyes,
so he can't soften.
No mouth,
so he can't soothe.
Blind and dumb like me.

I scream to deaf ears.
I run
down endless roads
to nihilism.

I weep impotence,
beg, plead and pray.
Yet the faceless, soulless man
stands rigid,
blocks my way.
Unbending – he too is bound by bureaucracy.

Dubai, January 1988

Beach cycle

Refresher sea
replenish me,
remove my sin,
revitalise my skin.
The shadows lengthen until I am no more than a rock.
The sea is blue.
The sea is green.
The foam is cleanest by the shore.

And as the sun
goes from yellow to gold
it dips and swells,
becomes the backcloth
to black boats and gulls,
blinds me.
Brazen flame of orange
now tips the ocean.
The sea is grey.
The foam is silver.
The sun now palest platinum.
The sky from rose to pink then blue,
striped as shadows on the sand.
Tequila sunset.

Now gone.
Yet the magic stays,
my smile repainted,
brow smooth, pain soothed.
I sit and watch
the space you left behind,
the glow your epitaph
and your prologue.

After the night
a fresh day will come to take my smile
and furl my brow.
Come evening.
Renewal.
Return to joy.

Dubai, February 1988

Fujeirah

Black sand
before a backdrop
of crude-chiselled stone,
dominant yet reticent,
softly masked in mist
or mirage.
Stolid beneath
millennia of unstinting sunshine.
Slices of silhouettes
stand each in relief
as a balanced deck of cards.
One tap to topple backwards to a dream.
And closer
a solitary scrub tree,
sentries the summit
of a near rock.
Leafless yet tall he stretches,
shoulders wide,
to fill the barren landscape
with his eye.
Switchback with me
down to Dibba
and south.
The mountains drink from the sea,
some paddle,
many swim waist high,
making homes for shoals
and spines or sharks,
burst with coral in their skirts,
dress their hair with birds.
The yawning bay is swept with sand,
speckled with seashells
and horizoned tankers
await their turn in tidal traffic jams.

Fujeirah, April 1988

Pattaya

Brash Blackpool with a twinkle
in its almond eye, flashing in the dark.
Single men with lust-drunk gaze
smile at girls with sharpened knives
and orchid breath. To softly tempt
the lonely hearts.

Dawn brings bawdiness and trash,
cheapness oozes from the cracks
between market stalls.
Jeep lights beckon, buses hoot
and beachy sunshades have a price.

Stones among the coarse crass sand,
stagnant pools that fish reject,
Thai-spiced skewers grilled
on kerbsides. Watch-sellers
strategically stand outside
the Bureaux de Change,
faking the time of their lives.

Thailand, May 1988

Phuket

Lush luxury.
Jungle clicks and whirrs
deafen glad ears,
surf, switchback
flips the seashore,
swapping calm for swell.

Rustic huts
cling and tangle in the forest.
Real shacks
line the puddle tracks,
stilted and patched
with seethrough halls
that are their homes and market stalls.
Women hunker on low platforms,
children sleep on wooden beds,
dogs lie flat with glazed eyes,
flickering in the dust.

The purple hue of pineapples
bursts between the coconut palms.
Rubber trees stretch up from their cup.
Bananas wave their flapping fronds
and pop with hands of fruit.
Amber sound winds muddily around the hills,
swooping to disclose a view
close to paradise.
A bay with arms outstretched in welcome
invites snorkellers to break some waves
and share the seashells
that abound.

Thailand, May 1988

Thai sounds

Pot pourri of cacophonies,
jumble din and jungle song
coloured by the beauty
of a silent orchid
and sweetly smiling,
cunning girls.

The hush and lap and smash
of aquamarine heaven.
The engine whirr
as leg rubbing, the screams
defy the sea's attempt
at drowning all remaining sound.

Chirrup and click of unknown
kingdoms high in humid undergrowth
and lowly, earthdumb snails
burrow into soundproofed sandsafety
and deeper still the coral crackles
to burst blazing and waving,
beckoning and laughing at strangers.

Tap tap tap goes the beaters' hammers,
bashing silver for their bread,
melting precious minerals,
trapped into the tourist trade
and blinded by button-popping snap hungry
bellyful trippers.
Bang clatter bang bang.
Thirty chisellers floor-squatting,
gouge their livelihood from
patterns in the teak.

Thailand, May 1988

Karachi

Dust-dulled garb hunkered blankly down
on chipped imperfect pavement slabs.
Straw between the rising cracks
of scrabbled life among the shacks.

Past freedom old colonial, such splendour
now collapsed and frayed. No room
for beauty under military rule.
The people wear weak smiles beneath
the heavy sun. Their city pitiless
and unadmired, no respect
for humankind, no pride
remains in what they've lost.

Bruising cloth against the stone,
rubbing, slapping, wringing a living.
Washermen and washerboys peg rupees in
the flagging breeze, their bloodstained
teeth adorn the smile that hides
the drug numbed mindlessness of moneymaking.

Downtrodden fruit rots in the gutter,
trampled by aimless sandaled feet.
Brimming drains and scattered remnants
of the beauty none perceive.

Oh the talent of the craftsmen,
tanning, tailoring their clothes
stitching, weaving, forging patterns.
A living looms up from the skein.
Brass and rosewood team
with onyx to bring the brazen bazaar
booty for the buyer's market;
crowds the tourist out with choice.

Yet the goodness waits in darkness,
way behind the crass façade
of prodding, staring, begging,
shouting, hooting, thieving,
democracy-hungry men
and children, signs and hoardings,
graffiti, dust and disrepair,
crumbling exterior, declining interior.
Discarded city without a home.

Pakistan, May 1988

60

Homesick

My thirst is quenched by exercise,
my sadness quelled by work.
Yoga is used to chain my mind,
imprisoning my thoughts.

I long for the chill of evening.
I dream my lungs are cool,
to exchange prickly heat for chilblains,
to shiver by the pool.

Oh the freedom of the walk,
striding forward
to flush out dust,
to stretch my limbs.
No direction
but movement.

What if the rose could bloom for me?
From bud to wilting,
weary head.

What if the scent
of pot pourri
were alive for me not dead?

What if the birds
could call my name,
the sparrows cheep
and doves deign
to bill and coo?

What if I were
inspired by sand?
What if the dunes
became my gods?

What if I could sing again?
What if I saw the good
that lurks behind my obsession?

For here nightlife
comes in cans,
culture comes on tape.

Daydreams ebb and flow,
eternal jetsam on
the shore of boredom.

I may never love again
a land more than my home.
a homeland filled with problems,
yearnings and despair.
For me the fires will always burn,
stoked by family and friends
by familiarity and ease
of acceptance.
The flames will be my muse.
They dance and beckon,
tempt and tease,
taunt relentlessly
knowing I am weak.

Dubai, June 1988

Solution

Loneliness is not physical
but an empty throbbing goal,
gaping and forlorn,
anticipating nought but lethargy.

Oh the effort of the push
and impetus to motivate
and eliminate my void.

Fill my objective,
remove objections,
weakly flung to mask my apathy.

Grant me strength
to forge the path to a new summit.
That I may climax with the joy of life
and that's enough.

Dubai, June 1988

Essentialism

I smile
and writhe,
activated by demand
and dirhams clocking by.

I rise on weakened arms
to shoulder from my prostrate pose
to knees.
At last I stand
tall enough to see the world
objectively below.
Less obstructive now,
more yielding than I then believed.

For it's I who must
overcome the barriers
to transcend bureaucracy
and join the Norfolk lark
I knew before.

It's I who must the effort make
fling the jetsam out to sea
and bid the waves come break with me
to roar and rage and race with me
that I may ride upon Arabian surf
and lose my thirst for Saxon turf.

The lark will not descend,
nor must I try to tempt it down.
Instead I must discard drab feathers
and don a positive garb
to join the life I knew before
among the scribes and scholars
I admire,
at one with the essential me.

Dubai, July 1988

Reboxed

The box is now,
sliding slyly across the world
to net me like a butterfly
unwillingly caged in paradise.

Its Perspex polished by a thousand slaves,
so clear I crash against it
and bang
it shocks me from my dream.

Ambitions struck down by the box
that puts me in between
my dreams and those of others
who tap contentedly towards Friday.

I need to grow.
Each achievement to flower.
Reminders of success.
We cannot cope without rain.
The piped water cannot permeate my box.
I lie parched and confused,
staring at the sun,
thirsty for the ocean drops
that keep me sane.

And then the floods seep beneath the crystal walls
and drown my time.
The dam so swiftly burst
is slowly mended.
The box no longer saturates my mind.
Drought returns.

Fowles came visiting.
Like Miranda I'm enshrined.
Like poor Koko I am blind.
Yet closer to the magic gift
of the father

I can write my way out of it.
My arms may be tied,
my mouth bound with tape,
but the words in my head
will worm themselves free
little by little.
I can dig the tunnel
Miranda failed, but
I shall not even break my nails.

Dubai, October 1988

Bookworm

Zigzag down the educated page,
eyes flit from piercing truth
to reflective thought.
The sentences a circus
of thrills and tears.

A flash wrenches at my heart
causes my mouth to flirt
with change in mood.

A narrow alleyway leads from the page,
backwards in time
I falter,
tiptoe from my words
to explore my own deep-seated truth.

An open plain,
pitted and hillocked
stretches from the ginnell strewn with memories,
flung aside til now.
A man like that.
A feeling empathised.
A walk
or conversation.
Narcissism from the page.

Dubai, November 1988

Hatta pools

Beauty at its most brutal.
Time's spurs like claws
scrape down the mountains,
duskily donkey brown
and cracked rubble scattered
with shrapnel shrouds,
sentinel to the peace within its womb.

Mirage made magical.
Still our pool unmirrored
in our recollection,
Proud pampas
reaches up in praise.
Delicate face
on a cruel landscape.

A lurking frog
cowers in his gulley,
croaks panting in the soaring heat.
His estate our solace,
cool between our toes.

Stacatto scrub.
Adagio day.
Pizzicato pools.
Punctuation
complements
the unrelenting sun.

Crystal water,
cupped by giant hands of stone,
tenderly held calm,
enshrined by lime-striped fists and jigsaw domes.

Plunge with me!
Dive from high
to where the waterfall
chatters with the inky depths.
White deluge
smashing black silk filled pool.

We swam and marvelled at the cool
smoothness of the walls
that clasped our silent sea.
Now blue.
Now clear.
Now aquamarine.

And into the light,
emerging from our dream,
we dive-bombed rockpools,
drowned the day in silt.

A twist and thrust
into a winding watery glade
that led us to an unknown end.

Rock furrows,
soon drenched by spring,
now stretched and bleached
by June.
Languid shadows lick
parched tongues
towards the dying pools
to drink and live again.

Hatta, November 1988

Hatta dunes

Red gold mounds of palpable
silence furled and furrowed,
sprigged with green,
deeprooted in the baking dust of a million
years of sunbasked, sunstopped solitude.
Vast sky presses down upon the sand,
bluely burdening the backs of stoic dunes.
The climb, such power in the heart of the machine.
A breath poised on the peak
then plummet softly as a bird,
song-free from relief.

The push and struggle,
jolts and perfect peace
atop the atoll, miles around
spot mountains, purple, chalk or
shifting with the sandy tide.

At nightfall the desert starts to frown
upon the fools who battle on,
torn between bold beauty and the risk of doom.

Hatta, December 1988

The camel

The camel, snooty and knock-kneed,
stands calmly while a caressing breeze
ruffles her doey lashes.
She lowers them to cast a casual glance
towards her newly born, who
so recently stood on slippery legs,
soon dried and dusted by the sand.

She lifts her graceful head,
still slowly to the umbrella of the acacia tree.
To gently tease a vagrant leaf, to softly tug
and flick its welcome moisture
to her mouth with practised ease.

So cool the camel and her young,
now arch their yearling necks milkwards
as she continues the graceful curve up
to the tip and curl of those dreamy eyes.

Dubai, May 1989

Jazirat al Hamra

Wooden doors bang back
against the brittle stone
with hollow sound;
the squeak of rust
upon the weakened hinge.
Some hang limply
or are cast aside.
The patterns scratched deep
into the sunbleached teak.
Diamonds, stars and moons
in praise of Allah,
or a more simple God?
Of survival in a land of searing heat
and scalding dust.
Cruel dryness,
parched lives beside the sea,
which stretches out to save them.
Yet surrender was the only step.
They left their well
to fill with stones.
The shady tree to shelter
just above the ruins
of their lives.
Roofs of laced palm
and floors of crushed rock,
coral patterns crumbling walls.
Like Orador Sur Glane, without the ravages of fire and war.
Yet still the discarded car
adorns the square.
And still the bicycle wheels, the post and pans
as if their own Hiroshima, Pompeii.
The cool sanctity of the crude minaret
beside the mosque,
now profane; broken
glass and empty cans mark Mecca.
And amidst the silence, where no birds have strength to sing
the forgotten doors clang weakly
to show their soul survives.

Ras al Khaimah, May 1989

Blighted ovum

So many questions
only answerable by time.
So long to wait
to grow, to ache.
And all those questions
ever rattling, poking fun at my weakness.
Why no omniscience?

I have the books.
Pages of problems solved,
hypotheses and hang-ups.
I know the numbers
of all the men
and women in the know,
the ones who've been through this.
The mental agonising
I endure.

A human's growing in my womb.
I'm filled with joy, with love,
with hope.
I'm panicking.
Each little twinge,
the minor aches of head
of limb, of abdomen.
And those darkening spots
of blood.

I'm scared.
I rest.
I'm bored.
So I'll just dwell on things that may
or won't or could someday.

Post script
Dilation and curettage.
A warm slap in the face
and the sick reassurance
that I'm the one in ten.
We'll face the facts
And try again.

Dubai, June 1989

Love song of a reluctant expatriate

I will always love you.
Despite time and distance.
For when I'm told to close my eyes
and picture a summer's day
it is you whom I turn to.
It is you I paint with boldness
behind my eyes.
You I see
when I am lonely,
blue and emerald,
yellow with buttercups,
grey and mean,
scratched black with leafless trees.
You I see parcelled in snow
or brushed with the syrup
of morning sun.
You and only you
with scattered villages
plump, sheep-peppered hills
that dip and fold
like velvet flung aside.

I love you,
though you may be poor
and bitter,
diseased with deprivation,
sick with grief.

I love you.
Despite the tattered cloth
within your belt of green.

I love you.
With my family in your pockets,
my soul in yours.
I'll be yours in time.

Dubai, June 1989

After it's gone

The words like Intercity 125s
scream round my head
without destination or intent,
save my distress
in this abyss.
With sleep my only solace.
Yet the dreams
are punctuated with restlessness,
I turn my back
away from thoughts
that will not stop.

I am a number.
One in ten.
A twenty-five per cent.
Once two
now none.
First fusion
then fission.
First exaltation
then depression.
One day in bed.
Fifteen minutes under.
Six weeks before a period.
Three months before
we try again.

Dubai, June 1989

Land of the tiger

Traveller's palms stretch up
in a wide smiling embrace
and give no shade from very sunny Singapore.
No longer stincapoo
but washed with sticky sweetness,
heady from frangipani
holding laughingly cupped hands
upwards to the sun.

Bamboo slim buildings
reach for the sky
to touch it lovingly.
For down among the bouncing crowds
lies perfection.
Proud white colonial past
wrapped in bougainvillea
as a gift for the future.
And Stamford stands nonchalant,
back to the sea,
ignoring sampans.

An island with its fingers
reaching out and up with promises
and hopes of happiness.
Inside its shores
all voyagers find a home.
In Raffles, the Long Bar or
Palm Court, where by candlelight
and white piano
they're lulled to inspiration and reflections
of Maugham and Conrad, even Coward
left their memory as epitaph.
Their works compiled, they say
beneath that tree, beside that palm.
And Princess Grace, the Lords, the Queens
have all shared the same beds
and punkahwallahs,
sipped that inevitable Sling.
A time when it was us and them
Depending on the colour of your skin.

Singapore, July 1989

76

The waiting room

Bleak and without walls
yet still enclosed, I wait
with suitcase packed,
lips clenched, unsure if it's worth
commencing conversation with the lady on my left,
or the smart girl on my right.

Few know when their train
will come.
Least of all me.
But how I long to go.
And how I dread to leave
behind our fortunes and the warm waves of weekends,
long days of sun.

It's not a case of waiting
for the train.
It's always there,
leaving many times a day.
So simple.
But when will we afford to switch a life of hope
for a taste of our dreams?
It all boils down to evil,
mind-obsessing gold.
Strung round our necks and wrists
like manacles.

The famous Golden Handcuff.
That's us.
And all the thousands of golddiggers who come here
month on month.
Like us they dig
Each monthly paycheque
brings them a little
closer to that cottage
in Provence.

Then bang! No sooner is the dream achieved
than it explodes with logic.
Without the safety of this dollar-growing desert
they dare not step out into the cold.

Dubai, October 1989

Sam and the sea

It was the kind of late afternoon
that adverts are made of.
Shadows lengthened
and the hush of the stretching sea
chased our bare feet
then ran away.

You walked in the tyre tracks
felt the peaks with your small feet,
placed them into adult footprints
claiming they were Daddy's.

Then I buried your toes
and you laughed
then buried mine.
I drew a fish with a stick.
You used it to make soft sand fly.
I used it to make spiralling holes
for you to fill with broken shells.

We watched an Indian take a swim
in his underpants
and later he asked you to pose with him
for a photograph on my camera.
You had sand on your face and held your stick tall.

And when you took my hand
to help you climb the hills that
only reached my calf
I felt my heart leap so
you could have been
my lover.

Dubai, November 1992

For Joshua

Our eyes spark
then fuse into a starburst.
Your first smile.
Mine.
Your full, fragile lips
quiver, purse, contort.
My heart flips and falters.
Your frown is mine
your happiness a quick empathy.
I will grow with you,
as I grew with Sam
as there in your hearts
I find myself.

Dubai, November 1992

The train stopped
when you were born

No timetables.
No suitcase.
Just carrying the joys and pain of each busy day.
No city suit.
No silent scream.
No rats, no scratching at the pane that shut me from my dreams.
I have no dreams and with them fled my muse.
The poetry is now.
Today my verse.
Yesterday a mere preamble to the truth.
A dream I'd never dared to hold.
It seemed too simple.

To be a mother
takes away the empty space
I filled with fantasy and black, bleak half-truths.
Introspection bred rejection of todays.
First Sam with trepidation
made his marks deep in our souls.
Now Josh has joined him
so our tomorrow is today.

Dubai, November 1992

OMAN 1993 – 1996

New Year's Eve

Star-studded Seifa.
Phosphorosence on the sand.
Waves of foam hurl at the shore,
flinging colliers de perles,
strings of diamonds.
Razzle dazzle in the sea.
Make spangled footprints,
then bejewelled soles.
Clap hands
for finger fireworks!

The yawning sea
said hush and sleep
as a blackened dome
swelled and winked
with starry pinpricks
overhead.

Our fire spat and crackled
but each flying spark
lifts up to decorate the sky.

The unexpected amber moon
tipped the horizon,
head askew
to unfold one open arm
of golden moonlight.
The arm grew slender
as it rose and paled
to glow and light the sky
and wave the firmament goodbye.

Seifa, December 1993

Sam's first day at school

They said you'd cry
and I would too.
And we did
at the same time
yet apart.
They held you from me as I left.
Such good, kind people.
And Kasey and Charlie were there.
Two friendly, familiar faces
in a sea of fear,
where painting, drawing,
singing, puzzles and fun
sat side by side
amid the foam and froth of
worry that Mummy will not come.

And when I did
you were there
wearing a stranger's shorts
and a proud grin.
You'd made it.
I nearly burst with joy.
My brave, my beautiful,
my cleverest of boys.

You sat beside Aunty Esther,
First teacher, a friend.
You called her Alastair.
With a pink piece of paper over your head,
you sang 'I shall sing a rainbow'
then you raised your arms
to catch two stars
and joined in Twinkle Twinkle.

Muscat, January 1994

My Daddy

On the day of my birth
you puffed on the stairs
while mother panted,
Chloe sneezed
and the midwife ranted.

When I first rode a bicycle
you held me until
I hit that lamppost.

You fetched me from school
and drove me up
to university,
walked me down the aisle.
Always there for me.
Always listening.
I mean really listening.

Caring, sharing my pain
and your enthusiasm,
face bright with youth.
You raise your finger
and grasp a point.
Omniscient almost.
'Daddies are magic'.
Once.

Now I understand
you are not infallible.
Now I appreciate
how well you did your job.

Your mind has always been
electric. Your walk
clumsy, your shyness
incomprehensible.

Always with me.
Every grey head is you.
My son's blue eyes
are yours.

You have your wish,
and though I pray
you will find fame
in paperback.
You are immortal.

Muscat, January 1995

Why we procreate

No lens can capture
soft white down on childish cheek,
blond hair like silken thread,
clear blue eyes,
lips pink and moist
or pale like soap flakes.
The flush and shine
of baby skin,
the tiny teeth
that twinkle when you grin.

And when that squishy
bit of of upper thigh
fades into your strong brown leg,
we smile with pride
and then we sigh
and wonder
if to do it all again
will make those childhood moments
just a little more lasting
more permanent in our busy minds
that sadly soon forget.

Muscat, January 1995

Contrast

Happy.
The humidity is gone.
The air sweet with petunias,
their faded frills unseen,
their straggled limbs
become a slender neck.
Frangipani, thick and tender,
buttermilk and gold
the scent as fat as cheese.
Palm trees open their hands
to praise the empty sky.
Children laugh.
A guitar plays.
The smell of peeled orange
cuts the air with tart tang.

Sad.
The pavement hard
beneath my feet,
my lungs pained by the fumes
of acrid oil, burning
to further heat the angry sky.
The flowers loll their tongues in
thirst,
trees supplicate the sky for cloud
to block the blue.
Cars breeze past.
Children cry.
Orange peel is littered on the kerb,
a misshapen twist of endless
circling into nothing.

Muscat, April 1995

Sri Lanka

The squeak of bare feet on dark terracotta floors.
The constant creak of kitchen doors
flipping waiters in and out.
Tuktuks cough and pop upon
the once made roads.
Drums play and the cornemuse.
Dancer's flikflak,
monkeys chatter on the tiles.
Cars hoot when they overtake,
while elephants shuffle as they drag
their fishtail branches
in the jungle.

Here in the heart of Ceylon,
on the veranda
of a planter's bungalow,
the tea trees quilt the hills
that pour before us
down and to the sea.

The only sounds are of silence.
Rough wind in the trees,
clattering twigs launch
like javelins into the lawn.
A pigeon calls,
another washboard rasps in pain,
some bicker, some complain.
A coo, a trill,
high-pitched starter motors.
Birds divebomb from the sky
like weighted leaves.

The women pick pick in silence,
smiling on the slopes to work.
Quiet sandals of young children
just the pluck and snap of
one bud and a pair of leaves.
Then the drying, rolling, withering,
ferment then sieve and pack.
The rising sun sends rays
of Orange Pekoe dawn.
The tea that starts the day for us
prolongs the toil for them.

Sri Lanka, May 1995

The beet field

Surreal Sam.
Two red dots
on the parched strip
between green beets
like mob caps.
Green gold corn
a dot of poppy
and the crush of camomile
beneath our sandaled feet.

Old Mother Rambler
marched on,
her white hat pulled down tight.
Young Master Whingebag
clung to Daddy's shoulders
and Sam raced on with PopPop
to the ploughed field
and the vast shade of the tree.

Thigh-deep they waded in the calm,
blossom-scattered, weed-skimmed Welland.
No minnows for tea
but sausages for lunch.
A rush basket
with two slots for wine.
A cork in the Puy Saint Servain
soon lifted
like the sun,
warm and smooth.
A snapshot day
to the river
and back.

Rutland, June 1995

Dates

An open mind.
An open door,
receptive,
waiting,
palms upwards.
Ripe landscape.
Opportunity comes
in bunches,
succulent, fresh and crisp
but juicier when dried.
A treasure in a wrinkled skin
with longboat pips
and sprays fat as goats' udders.
Yellowed or ruddy
their soft acorn cups
fat as lilac,
heavy as wisteria,
worthy of purple.
We ripened together
as they fell in our laps
and into our hands,
made a date with the page
and became our legacy.

Muscat, September 1995

You are what you eat

Fat makes fat.
Butter on my thighs,
banana muffins
on my bum.
Why I ate that éclair was not clear.
Sugar makes me sweet, honey.
Not so sweet to my sweet.
I never eat oranges,
so why am I covered in their peel?
They don't appeal to me.
If I liked string beans
would I become one?
Sort of green
with bumps zippered down my front?
I guess I must have eaten too many pears.
Or grapes.
Sour grapes.

Muscat, September 1995

On hearing the news

Stunned into seeing things again -
the way mountains stand against the sky
as if cut out with scissors.
A green and orange scarf
floats diagonally behind a flipflop shod lady,
straight-backed, grey-haired,
balancing a bag of hay on her head.

The turbans twisted,
embroidered caps,
bare feet,
brown eyes,
henna-tipped fingers,
toes and wrists that swirl
with flowers.

Suddenly the beauty
leaps out and grabs me by the throat.
Choked,
the well fills up
with things to do,
to paint, to write
to see again
to be again.
One last time.

Last night the beach,
dappled with artificial light,
was pale and pitted,
as if I looked down on the whole empty quarter.
Wahiba Sands.
Each dimple was the sink in my heart,
each dune tip – the thought I must record before it goes.

The black sea sliced
by a white boat.
A furrowed vee,
like combed hair
and the sky so dark,
stopping sharply
at the sea's horizon.
A light flashed out from Fahal Island.
Set the cliffs on fire.

Breeze fresh, my tears new.
Hush said the tiny bubbles,
popping sadly on the shore.
Be calm.
I'll be there for you in Stavanger.
Same sky.
Same sea.
Same same?
I think not.

Muscat, October 1995

Dusk in Qurm

The pulse and push
of runny honey
to the shore.
The globe of sun
dips and dies
behind the cliff.
The minaret splutters
and the Mullah sings.
Another call to prayer.
Another dusk.
Another tug at my heartstrings.

A flat boat,
black against the silver sea.
A boy kneels at the bow
then lies flat
and disappears.
Only his heels twitch
as he hauls up a fish.
The boat slides
from the bay.
The boy slides back
into the sea.

Muscat, October 1995

Lest I forget

Bougainvillea the colour of barley sugar,
old lace or 70's plum.
An old man's beard, wide and white
as an open palm.
Dishdash the colour of camel,
khunjar slung across thin hips,
skirt hitched to show anklebones,
brown sandals, dusty feet.
The blue-tipped wings of a roller
skim across the sky,
dip behind a palm tree.
Out of sight.
Little fat partridge waddles across the road
too scared to fly.
A lark sings in the wadi.
A grey heron, owl-like, hunches shoulders in the park,
then wide-winged he flies
to fan the air like Nature's punkahwallah.

Muscat, November 1995

Pox envy

Sam has eighty-nine spots so far.
It's day three
of chickenpox.
He has a spot
in his throat
and it hurts.
He says he's
An 'a Hundred-and-One-Dalmation'.
Brave boy.
And he's glad.
Josh only had thirty.

Muscat, December 1995

Dread

Sick pit in my stomach.
Please stop talking
of Norway.
I don't want to go.
It's not Norway
that's to blame –
despite a sea of cool,
fat prawns, raw carrots
and brown cheese.

Despite the cold, the dark,
the cost of a car.
No matter how much
you tell me of snow,
the skiing,
wooden floors,
effective central heating
and soft, Shetland-coloured hills.
It's not home.

For home is where my heart is,
where I have friends, or family, or both.
For home is where my hearth is,
where I have permission to belong.
My pubs, my high street, smoking fire,
my wedding presents, my church spire.

Muscat, December 1995

Take me

Take me.
Pluck me from my home
and friends.
Drag my children from their school
and familiar ways.
Wrest me from my bank account.
Tear me from the things I know
and fling me, emptied, licked clean
of local knowledge
to a place that will be barren,
despite its mountains,
dry, despite its fjords.
Push me into the faceless crowd
that I may take those faltering steps,
a child beneath each arm.
Wide eyed and fearful,
all of us.
Pay us well and we will not complain.
Then close the door.
Slam it.
I know you do.
Yet you will never change me,
nor mould me to your ways.
I will never bow to your superiority.
I will never be your slave.
You can rob me of my home,
steal my family, take my friends,
but you will never have my soul.
So handcuff us to dollar signs,
bind our feet and hands,
but you will never close my mouth
nor quell my dreams of pleasant lands.

Muscat, December 1995

A silence you can touch

Calm in the basket.
A blast of fire,
blue-fringed and feathered,
like dragon's breath,
puffs the balloon
and we rise towards heaven.
So still but for the rush of flames,
Sometimes nothing but a drift
in a sky of tranquillity
and a silence you can touch.

Sand speckled with scrub,
dots green on beige.
Piebald mountains,
from the scattered,
swelling cloud.
Black on grey.
Pale rock.
Veined land.

Now we fly,
light as the wind
that no-one feels.
Soft now
as smiles lick our lips
touch our upturned faces,
display a waking world.

The camels do not raise
a disinterested eyebrow,
while goats scud
and young boys gather,
locust-like from nowhere.

No tigers here.
No wildebeest.
Just a bowl of mountains,
cupped in a shy embrace.
Engulfed and consumed
by a silence you can touch.

Muscat, January 1996

Moving on

From disbelief
to sadness.
A trickle of hope
begins to fill a well
then dries.
We smile the smile
of the helpless,
fill packing cases
with our lives
and litter today with regrets.
We pack up our wooden memories,
our celluloid and prints.
But friendship is harder to leave
and impossible to take.

And so we have
one last cocktail or barbie,
one last call,
one last time.
We live in a limbo
of tied ends and throwing out
and too many goodbyes.
Nothing happy happens
when you're packing.

The gannets descend,
open-pursed,
button-mouthed.
And we slide down the slope
in a forest of mire.

When we step on the runway
and the end is in sight,
no pit could be deeper.
Though things will improve,
please God can you stop them
from making us move
again?

Muscat, January 1996

Gone

Gone.
The eau de nil
of soft lawn folds
from shallow triangle of yoke.
The twisted cashmere turbans
and layered peacocks without veils.
Gone the easy Indians,
the cultural bouillabaisse,
the nods and smiles and shaking heads.
Gone the motorway furniture
in fibreglass, the fountains
and the recent past.
Gone the beauty,
skeined in yellow flowers up to Seeb.
Up, away, off.

We float
in a dream that still holds
the not quite truth
that we have moved.
Yet Julie's tears were real enough,
our house an empty shell.
Occasional turbulence
but not enough emotion.
It's still not true.

A decade
streams away.
Strip of sand fades with greygreen palms.
The rugged range vanishes
into a vacant sky,
becomes a distant star
to wink with memories.
And as we soar
our spirits plunge.
We try to trap the vapour trail
and save it in a jar.
We fail.

Muscat, January 1996

NORWAY 1996 – 1997

New anonymity

From someone
to no-one.
My ego in a packing case
bound for Norway
from Oman
where I knew fame
and it knew me.
Who'd choose invisibility?

Can cash compensate
for an identity
that's boxed up forever?
Memories of being loved
become ornaments
and videotape.
And as the snow plough
forces new furrows,
so must we.
Snow is not sand
despite similarities.
Herring is not hammour.
Larva mountains
not bedrock.
We'll change our needs
and find new friends.
But does money really make amends?

Ian was a rock star.
Sam and Josh were teachers' pets.
I was an author.
Let us not forget.

Stavanger, February 1996

At thirty–five

I learned the truth at thirty-five
that I was made to be alive
to watch the sunlight stripe the trees,
see lichen green and rusty leaves.
And now I know I am a writer,
glad I learned it now, not later,
found the value of the pen,
the joy I give to all of them
But most of all it's me I'm pleasing
and my joy is still increasing
with each bud of coming spring
I'm looking hard and listening.
I'm glad to be alive
at thirty-five.

Stavanger, March 1996

Searching for sunshine

Another pine tree
moves starched petticoats
through the crowd
of taller cones.
Lost in transition.

A lonesome pine.
Alone.
Green anonymity
without strings
or floats.
Black ice of foreign land,
planing, drifting.
Lost.
Not wanting to be found.

And now the first buds are tipped with gold.
Spring fairy lights
in the forest.
Dripping from those petticoats,
pearls of rain,
like tears on noses,
tears in eyes.

Forsythia the sunshine,
bright against the wood.
A pox of dandelions
on the landscape.
Pompoms spot the green.
Oak leaves unfurl their golden fingers
to brighten the moods and woods,
beeches burnish.
Take pride and passion in the reds
and froths of lace on hedgerows.
Beads on bushes will turn merry
as the summer's feast finds blueberries.
Streams chuckle, children splash,
the lizard sighs and breathes
its shallow breath.

A gentle push and pull
of ageing skin
in soft wrinkles
to and from the shore
to lap a little like spilt beer
with headless, open-bubbled foam
against the lichen splashed
flat stones.

Popbeads, bladderwrack and strap
the ruddy belts of weed
glimmer in new light.
Pink thrift or white clover,
moss like fleecy coats,
feathered fronds,
spongy beneath my feet.

A textile lover's heaven
as out burst magical glades
and rocks and caves,
perfect for trolls.
Paradise for small boys,
lashing logs and climbing trees,
gullies fill with last year's leaves.

And on and up and through and round.
Another landscape
in a foreign land.

Stavanger, May 1996

Autumn

A day dipped in honey,
leaves round and smooth,
yellow as toffee pennies,
flat on the path.
Dank autumn undergrowth
sweet with coriander scent
of pine needles, pierce the air.

A search for fairy rings,
pale mushrooms, purple, black
or bracket fungus clinging to the trunks.

Streaks of sunlight,
flash gold across the flaming foliage
and deep green fir trees soar towards a dark blue sky.
White clouds float by, reflecting on
the rust and copper echoes in the fjord.

Stavanger, November 1996

Christmas is not mistletoe

Take Christmas warmth.
For you it may mean cheer,
warm laughter,
hot flames
or old flames.
For me the warmth is
of sunshine,
too hot to eat outside at midday,
but cool enough on the beach for cocktails.

Take Christmas presents.
For me it was 'who' was present.
Not 'what'.
A set of in-laws.
Mine or his.
Ten or even twenty friends -
new ones of course.
There are no old friends
where we've been.
No-one gets the chance.

Take tidings – of joy of course.
For me the tide rolled in
with the call to prayer
and left with a stripe of moonlight
licking the slate and silver sea
that twinkled with a million stars
and diamonds that danced
in the phosphoresence.

Take the morning service.
Not at the church, nor in the mosque
but served with a white smile
that sliced a nut brown face
and said 'Merry Christmas, Madam-Boss.'
Service even on Christmas Day,
so we could sit at long tables
in our bougainvillea-choked courtyard,
shaded by sticky-scented quisqalis,
jasmine and magnolia
joined by twenty strangers
having the time of our lives.

Stavanger, December 1996

One for joy

I shall miss the magpie,
who teeters and twitches
on the bullet-shaped chimney stone
outside our cross-paned
bedroom window.
Today it is spring
and he hops up there
to show me
how cleverly
he holds three twigs in his beak this time.
Last March he did the same,
black and white
against a shining blue sky,
pale and cold,
scarfed with a thin mist
of angel-hair cloud.
He bobs and jerks his tail
up and down
like a railway push-me-pull-you.
Each lift emits
a squeak of pride.
I no longer see one as sorrow
and I need not two for joy.
One is joy.

Stavanger, March 1996

The last writers' circle

Through a window
veiled by time,
I will see you all
like a fading memory.
Seated round a table,
clutching coloured cardboard folders,
pouring tea from a TV kanne.
Taking pastries from a plate.
You are smiling,
thrilled to be together again
for your fortnightly fix of inspiration.
It was my catalyst,
my lifebelt too.
The one rock of sanity
in that sea of anonymity.
I had floundered helplessly,
until I found you.

Through a window
veiled with hope
I can see you now,
gently changing the world.
Language your weapon,
your workhorse, your balm,
plucking thoughts from your sky,
to let lie in your palm.
Play with them,
dance with them,
waltz with the words,
then place them on paper,
slide onto the screen
and toss them to me.
Let me share your dreams.

Through my window
veiled by time,
I will look out to sea,
watching for your word-bunting,
hoping you will visit me.
Stay near me with your writing,
Our words will connect us
In spite of the miles.

Stavanger, May 1997

ENGLAND 1997 – 2004

Coming home at last

A Cider with Rosie summer.
A perfect Wordsworth day.
An Auden kind of sorrow
when we had to go away.
With Betjeman style Sundays,
though the lawns were brown,
we fed the ducks and stood and stared
in George Eliot's town.
Teenagers in uniform,
big boots now,
shaven hair,
still loll against treetrunks,
walk in threesomes,
cross the square.

Seventy-seven and it was me.
Hot summer term in upper fifth.
bold without my boater,
navy and white print dress,
bare legs and lonely heart.
I remember Wimbledon,
drawn curtains in the lounge.
A host of girls and my thankfully complicit mother.
We listened to Genesis and Pink Floyd and felt grown up.
We were back then.
But more so now.
The sky was just as blue,
but now my forehead's etched by a score of years
and a life between countries,
wrenched from hearth to humidity,
and to and fro and back again.
Cultural deserts.
Easton oasis.
Sanctuary at last.

Rutland, June 1997

114

Ten years

A decade of delight,
peppered with more joy
than cupid could aim for.
You give me love
you gave me boys
and more happiness
than I'd dare to hope for.

You are the sun that rises
on a palm-fringed shore,
the minaret that calls to prayer –
for God is great and so are you.

You are the phosphoresence
on my sea of memories.
The star that shoots
in my night sky,
my bright and vibrant bougainvillea,
my comical yet steady clown fish,
my sweet and tender date.

Dubai made me decide I loved you,
Muscat's music wrote our song,
Stavanger made us stronger still,
carving out our lasting bond
on the rocks we had become.
England now has proved your love
can grow in Easton-on-the-Hill.

You are my protecting arms,
my welcome chest,
my devil's advocate, my ear,
my solace when I have you near,
my muse, my optimist and fan.
You'll always be my action man –
the most beautiful man in my orchestra.

Rutland, December 1997

Summer morning in SW18

Blue-swiped sky.
Fat patches, bright between the roofs,
the leaves, the For Sale boards.
Birds chatter,
women call 'hello',
babies wrinkle their faces from the sun
and pierce the silence, as it is.

A helicopter circles
and I hear a distant drill,
pneumatic of course.
The scrape of shovel into wet concrete.
Next door they are building a wall.
Over the road some slabs turn into
offstreet parking.

A deep voice bellows in Spencer Road.
A door bangs shut.
An engine revs.
And then a splash of quiet
just wide enough for the leaves to rustle
before that blessed drill.
Again. Then a lorry's horn,
the clunk of planks on scaffolding.
The helicopter returns
to join the tinkle of a wind chime
caught by the breeze
that lifts the corners of my magazine.
London in the sun.

London, June 1999

Friends re-untied

I found you on the Internet
and think of times I'd not forget
when, smooth-skinned, we had been friends
and life and future had no end.
And today my head is filled
with things I'll leave unsaid until
the barrier of Broadband makes me bold
enough to write those words untold
and take the thoughts I'd put on hold
to foolishly unfold
the careful pleats
of days I'd put away
to save until another day,
like this, when memories are bliss.

Rutland, January 2003

THE NETHERLANDS
2005 –

My next mountain

Do it!
Do it for you!
Not just because -
but because you are
a mother, wife,
or because you can
or should.
For you.
Because one day
the nest will be empty
and then there will be you
alone.

Get a move on!
Move on up right now!
Don't waste time waiting,
killing seconds,
drowning minutes
and heaping sand upon the hours.
Don't waste those possibilities.
Not you,
you of all people!
You of such potential,
passion, drive, ambition.
Where is your lark now?
What apogee, what whim?
Even the lark would never swoop
so low.

Rise up!
Rise up again!
Remember how to soar?
Remember?
Where is your mountain now?
Beyond.

It lies beyond.
Way past comfort
and in the land of fear.
That's where.
That's why you dare not go.
But you know?
That's where your 'next' will be.

Believe!
Believe in you!

Voorschoten, October 2005

Keukenhof

. . . and the sails turn,
white stripes skim
each wooden arm, now slow,
now fast as the May breeze
touches new budding,
blossoming, pale frothed trees.
Lime leaves unfurl
from winter's cocoon.
A sea of magenta, apricot and scarlet
tulips with triangle tops,
face up to the sun.
The carillon by the mill rings out
anachronistic tunes of Alabama,
authentic songs of Amsterdam,
as people slop past,
pushing wheelchairs,
dragging dogs and children,
begging for ice cream.

Gypsy Queen, Roccoco, Juan, Sancerre
stand side by side in
swathed blocks of cushioning colour,
scattered artfully between the shrubs,
the beech, camellias and rhododendron,
Fritillaria stoop subserviently to
rise up above the humble hyacinth.

Lisse, May 2006

Spring clean

I will sit in the garden tomorrow and play
with the silence.
I'll mould it with my fingers,
palm it, cup it, toss it in the thickening air,
lean back into my wicker chair
and stretch my legs and mind.

First pay attention.
Call it 'Artist's Date'.
Plate up those tasty morsels
that muscle in when silence seeps
into each space.

A duck potters and swaggers
along the bank then plops
down with seven ducklings.
Green and gold among the daisies.

Sounds battle with scents
and sights
and the soft breeze
on my pale winter's cheek.

Then in wades recognition -
sparks that light a train of flashbacks,
half-remembered plans that teeter,
poised on the brink, totter
when they try to land.

Ripples float outwards,
fall back into the fusty space,
that's lost at the back of the cupboard of my mind.

Come into the garden!
Breathe in the new mown lawn,
thick lilac-scented, purple air.
Shake out your crumpled part-worn plans
and persevere with those that really please
now days are long and sunshine and iced wine
are no more the cloth of dreams.

Sit with me here
in this bliss of open space
and open mind.
Spring cleaning means
leaning back into the sun.

Voorschoten, May 2006

Unity in diversity

Connected cultures,
linked lifestyles
Women United –
unique and bold,
conjoined by our teacher
to set process and goals.

We chose colours and roles.
Came together
then split like the Hokey Cokey,
united, divided, but never alone.

First, we moved singly,
gently, with our separate squares,
each to our own tune.
We played our parts, apart, until
like Billy Elliot, we 'disappeared' into The Zone.

Then,
tentatively,
we fell into the Two Step
reaching for the one who held our head,
our limbs,
our hand.
Back and forth we danced and
soon became The Light Fantastic,
as dusk fell.
Matching, mending, mewling,
marvelling at magic we had made.

Until,
reassembled,
cheesecake and berry-filled,
we saw the wonder of creation.

Twelve paintings with a common hue,
Twelve dancers moving to one tune.
Twelve strangers sharing the same goal
Twelve artists going with the flow.
This was no Last Supper.

The Hague, July 2006

The healing

High on heels,
it feels better to teeter.
Taller now,
limbs lengthened,
shoulders back,
head high,
stretching upwards from my soul.
I grow.

See how I dance now,
living for today,
sleek as a languishing kitten,
I prance and flex my steps.
I'm smitten by my pointing toes,
they tip and totter, make me glow.
Kick up a dust.
Kick up my heels.
Kick start my golden mood.
I don my sexy slingbacks
and lose the need for food.

It may take a cobbler
to make a shoe
but heels make a woman
out of me.

The Hague, May 2006

Annie's magic

A time to write, a time to dream,
a place where girls unite, find themes
and soon forget their might-have-beens,
replacing them instead with words that heal
the gaping wounds that wind and twine round self-esteem.

For fear crushes hope, blinds us to a reality
that only others see, they say.
They say we're writers, every one.
No dead wood.
But even as such purple praise falls on our ears,
deafness sets in, for she who reads before,
or after, seems to win.
Only 'others' have the flair
that those agents long to snare.

Sitting pinkly in the window seat,
hugging knees and shrugging off those pleas that beg us to believe that
greatness is not far afield.
We lean against the pane
of glass that splits us from the lucky few
and hold this moment, captured, like a butterfly,
that flaps its wings, laced around with laughter.
Friendships, though fast, are made to last.
Six days of pure gold, finely spun into a web of wonder,
then dropped by piglets flying past,
clasped our castle in the park.

Then Annie, dressed in velvet, took out her magic wand,
made spells to quell our nervousness, made us believe we were the best.

May her sorcery sustain us when self-doubt comes to claim us.
May our love sustain her when health begins to pain her.
And may we never dare forget that we'll all be published yet.

Scotland, April 2007

Belly dancing

Chin high,
hip, thigh,
pointed toe and fingers wide.
Belly laugh,
belly roll,
lean back and flip your hair from side to side.
Sensuous circling,
pelvic floors tightening as
cat-like, caressing,
you brush your own cheek with your shoulder.
Chest up
and stretch that pink gold ballet shoe
that peeks out like a flicking tongue
from beneath the black gauze of a
silver-tasseled skirt.
Down, up, shake shake.
Down, up, shake shake.
Trace crazy eights above the wood,
as thrusting hips obey the tabla's
dom tukha tuk
and you snap
your back back
make your belly round
then flat
then crack it
back to base.

Layla, the teacher,
has a small tattoo on her smooth tummy
and a mobile phone curved into the crook of her shoulder.
She takes one dainty hennaed toe
and taps out the rhythm for you.
Upper body icy still,
her free hand like an eagle's wing.
Facing forward
she thwacks the floor with her sole.
It smacks like wet washing on a line.
She gently tucks her phone into her waistband.

The music mesmerises.
Tabla, sitar, cornemuse,
pipes and drums and cloven hooves.
It thrashes, writhes, it spins and whirls
as belly dancers reach and curl
until the throbbing dies,
as warm wind sighs on dunes at sunset,
whips veils across faces
and goats skip sideways to a safer place and calm
until a fall of rocks skitters down.
The women turn, then raise their hands to giggle,
hide their smiling lips and close their eyes,
coquettish now, not shy
as they raise their skirts, enter a trance
and slowly they begin to dance.

Dubai, May 2008

Busy

I'll find you in the garden,
your hands streaked black with soil,
poking fragile roots into trowelled holes.
Pushing fingers into autumn briars,
stain them red and black with berries,
loving all that grows
on ground and tree or in the hedgerow.

I'll find you in the country lane,
dog lead swinging from your pocket,
and you, deep in conversation with a neighbour, friend or postman
laugh oblivious to the escaped dog
and the car slamming on its brakes.
Clap your hands and whistle!
The Working Cocker trots closer,
feathers and ears flying
and you whelp with pride
as wet paws prick, sliding
muddily on your thighs.
'Good girl!' you say,
patting hard her silken back.
Her wagging tail seems fit to snap.

I'll find you by the pulpit,
buckets crammed with red and green,
bursts of yellowgold and cream.
Standing back, considering
the lilies on the font
in all their glory.

I'll find you at your easel,
low stool balancing on sand
as you paint the sea in pastels
drawing passion with your hand.

I'll find you on the swingseat,
lulled gently by a glass of wine,
eyes closed and face upturned
to the evening sun
that dips below the rooftops as
you sip the drink you've earned.

I'll find you on the sofa,
damp dog spooning at your side,
as your husband of fifty years,
my father, head flopped back like a hinge,
sleeps and snores. Silent, breathless
before each almighty explosion
that you just ignore.
You'd rather watch the flames of a living fire.
Jessie, pressed against you,
prods you with her paw.
You set down your tea
and stroke her willingly.

I'll find you in the mirror
when I trace the lines upon my face.
And I find you when my children
stoop to kiss you and embrace.
You're in my words, my lips, my head,
my love of cheese with fresh French bread.
At my shoulder by the stove,
reminding me that I should use
'five, three and two' for crumble,
'four, four and two' for cake.
You're in every dish I make
and blackened on the base of each burnt pan –
a memory that will not scrape away.

I find you there in every sigh
that's glad we'll have a sunny day.
'Oh boy, this'll do chaps'.
'This is just the job,'
as stripping off the layers of cloth
you turn your face up to the sun
and thank the Lord for what he's done.

Voorschoten, January 2009

About the author

Jo Parfitt has lived and worked as a writer in five countries during the last 21 years. She has written 26 non-fiction books, the most well known of which is Career in Your Suitcase. Recent titles include Expat Entrepreneur, Find Your Passion, Release the Book Within and a new edition of the cookbook she co-wrote in Muscat with Sue Valentine, called Dates. In 1985, her first book, French Tarts, was accepted by the first publisher she approached. Jo is a prolific journalist, who specialises in expatriate and career issues, a keynote speaker and workshop leader. An inspiring teacher and passionate mentor she loves to help those who want to get published and paid for it. Her motto is 'sharing what I know to help others to grow'. In 2009 she completed work on her first novel.

Find out more at www.joparfitt.com

www.ingramcontent.com/pod-product-compliance
Lightning Source LLC
LaVergne TN
LVHW021348080426
835508LV00020B/2175